Why Do I Do The Things I Do?

Understanding Personalities

Darrell J. Parsons

Parsons Publishing House
Your Voice Your World ™
Stafford, VA USA

Why Do I Do the Things I Do?—Understanding Personalities
By Darrell J. Parsons

Parsons Publishing House
P. O. Box 488
Stafford, VA 22554 USA
www.ParsonsPublishingHouse.com
Info@ParsonsPublishingHouse.com

This book or parts thereof may not be reproduced in any form, stored in a retrieval system, or transmitted in any form by any means—electronic, mechanical, photocopy, recording or otherwise—without prior written permission of the publisher, except as provided by the United States copyright law.

All scripture quotations, unless otherwise indicated, are taken from the New King James Version®. Copyright © 1982 by Thomas Nelson, Inc. Used by permission. All rights reserved.

Scripture quotations marked HCSB are taken from the Holman Christian Standard Bible®, Copyright © 1999, 2000, 2002, 2003, 2009 by Holman Bible Publishers. Used by permission. Holman Christian Standard Bible®, Holman CSB®, and HCSB® are federally registered trademarks of Holman Bible Publishers.

© 2011 by Darrell J. Parsons
All rights reserved.

International Standard Book Number:
13 digit: 978-1-60273-019-9
10 digit: 1-60273-019-9
Library of Congress Control Number: 012905463
Printed in the United States of America.
Published by Parsons Publishing House
for World-Wide Distribution.

Table of Contents

Preface	v
Acknowledgments	viii
Introduction	ix
1. The Beginning	1
2. Why Am I This Way?	5
3. Are There Others Out There Like Me?	11
4. The BIG 4	17
5. The "D" Personality: Direct & Demanding	23
6. The "I" Personality: Inspiring & Influential	29
7. The "S" Personality: Steady & Stable	35
8. The "C" Personality: Competent & Compliant	39
9. Put It in the Blender	43
10. I Am As God Has Made Me	49
11. Apostle Paul: Demanding, Decisive, & Doing	53
12. Apostle Peter: Impressive and Inspiring	59
13. Apostle Andrew: Steady, Stable, & Secure	69
14. Apostle Thomas: Cautious & Competent	75
15. Trust Keeps the Team Together	81
16. Mentoring & Discipling	87
17. The Transformative Personality	91
18. So Why Do I Do the Things I Do?	95

Preface

Wisdom is the principal thing; Therefore, get wisdom. And in all your getting, get understanding (Proverbs 4:7).

I have found that in my own life that understanding personalities has been a huge asset to my development as a husband, father, employee, and military officer.

In some aspects of my life, I am a leader, and in other aspects, I am a follower and knowing how to work with various personalities is wisdom to help me be a better leader and team member.

Leadership is all about influence and getting things done whether it is in the home, on the job, or with the kids. Everyone is a leader in some area of their life and everyone is a follower in another area. Navigating the world of leadership and followership can be challenging and frustrating. However, understanding personalities can be a key tool for navigating the rough waters of leadership and followership.

One of the keys to successful leadership is to develop the right team at the right time for the right job. Understanding personalities greatly helps in selecting the right team members whether your team is at work, at play, or just living life.

In this book, we will examine the DISC model for grouping personality traits. For example, my primary personality is the drill instructor which is an aggressive leader always looking for new challenges and attacking the task. However, the secondary part of my personality tones down my primary traits. With my Drill Instructor personality, I am more interested in the challenge of a new task, but not at the expense of the people around me. I'm a kinder, gentler person with the cushion of my secondary traits; at least that is my goal. We will seek to discover your primary and secondary traits as we proceed.

With knowledge of the DISC model, when I supervise a team or lead my class of 5th and 6th graders at church I seek to interact with the group based on the strengths of each personality. If I need a detailed person to determine a budget, I don't assign a people-person. If I need someone to greet people at church, I don't assign a number-cruncher.

The bottom line is two-fold: get the task accomplished and enjoy personal fulfillment for each team member. When we work with our personalities and our strengths there will be a greater level of personal success for all. It's a better world when we always endeavor to set others up for success.

I want to emphasize that your personality is a gift. Research shows that 85% of a child's personality is formed by the time they reach five years old. Genetics and experience work together to make you like you are. Let's start at the beginning of our journey to find the answer to why we do the things we do and what motivates others by understanding personalities. Looking through the Apostle John's eyes at his fellow disciples, we will begin our journey.

ACKNOWLEDGMENTS

This book is dedicated to my wife and partner for-life, Diane. Your "CS" to my "DI" makes us a perfect match.

I also dedicate this book to my daughter, Brianna—you bring happiness and joy to my life.

Special thanks to Dr. Mels Carbonell whose vision and teaching inspired this book.

Introduction

Everyone is gone. The other eleven have gone on to receive their rewards with the Savior. Martyrdom has claimed the ones that came later such as Paul and Mark. The Apostle John is the last remaining of the original twelve. Why did God choose these men? What was it that allowed them to endure all adversity—even to the point of death—and continue to build the church?

John remembers when Jerusalem was destroyed in 70 AD all too well. The Roman Empire had taken notice of the Christian Kingdom and decided to obliterate it and kill the last of the original apostles. However, the Apostle John does not die easily and the church only grows more and more.

Many accounts of Jesus Christ have circulated throughout the church. Some have been accurate, but not all. Not wanting to reproduce the writings of others, John surveys the church and prepares to bring forth a book directed by the Holy Spirit filled with new revelations. The year is approximately 90 AD, and the beloved disciple John begins to pen his own gospel.

While this fourth gospel does not explicitly identify its author, Irenaeus, the Bishop of Lyons, identified the author as the Apostle John; hence, church tradition holds that this gospel of John was indeed written by the Apostle John in the city of Ephesus.

The grand and glorious city of Ephesus was the capital of the Roman province of Asia, which is now part of western Turkey. When the Apostle Paul first visited this city around 52-55 AD, he found a large city filled with fame, power, superstition, and sin with its greatest claim to fame being the grandiose temple of Artemis or Diana, which later became one of the seven wonders of the ancient world.

Around 60-61 AD, Paul wrote a letter to the church in Ephesus to unveil the mystery of the glorious church. Later, he tells Timothy to stay in Ephesus, and church history records that young Timothy remained as the pastor of that church until his martyrdom in 96 AD. 1 Timothy 1:3 records Paul's charge, "As I urged you when I went into Macedonia—remain in Ephesus that you may charge some that they teach no other doctrine."

The church in Ephesus is solid and Timothy remains as the pastor. It is 90 AD as John writes his gospel; he thinks back to his brothers in the faith and surveys what an unlikely mix of characters were used by the Lord to establish His church. Peter was always good for a laugh. He always had a big smile on his face. He had a way of making people feel like they were his best friend. John also thinks of Peter's brother, Andrew.

So unlike his brother, Andrew was quiet and shy, but steady and stable. Where Peter would fall apart, Andrew would always keep things together. However, once Andrew got to know you, he would really warm up and talk and laugh as much as Peter. Peter was great in a crowd, but Andrew could always be seen working one-on-one ministering to people individually.

John begins to miss them all, even Thomas. He recalls how Thomas always got a bad rap for the time he questioned Jesus. John understood that Thomas' personality needed concrete proof in order to believe, and it didn't seem to bother Jesus. Jesus never rebuked or scolded Thomas for his need of proof. However, once converted, he was committed to the cause. Thomas was more like Paul than the other apostles in that once he set his mind and heart on something, he was unstoppable.

John recalls that when he first saw Paul, who was known then as Saul of Tarsus, at the Sanhedrin council in Jerusalem. There was nobody else like him. He was brash, arrogant, and always on the go doing something. It seemed as if Saul of Tarsus might be able to single-handedly destroy the gospel by arresting and persecuting the entire church. However, after Paul's conversion he spread the Gospel of Jesus across more nations than the rest of them combined.

John wonders about the diverse group of people that came together to be called the Apostles of the Lamb. Why were they all so different? What made each one so unique? Their personalities were completely different, but uniquely suited for the plan and purpose which the Lord had for each of them individually and for the group as a whole.

With this backdrop, the Apostle John writes his gospel—the good news about his close friend and Savior, Jesus Christ. John recalls the words of Jesus and decides to start at the beginning which allowed him to connect Jesus to the beginning of all time. John begins his book with the same three words that the book of Genesis starts with, "In the beginning..." Now, we will start at the beginning.

1

THE BEGINNING

Have you ever done something and wondered, "Why do I do these things?" Have you ever stopped trying to do something, only to repeat it again and again and again? You get the picture. During those times, have you ever wondered, "Why do I do that?" If you can answer yes to any of these questions, then this book is for you. The good news is that you are not alone; there are others out there experiencing these things just like you! That really is good news!

This is NOT a book of psychoanalysis or a seven step process to fix you. This book comes from over 20 years of observation and study of how people react and why they do it. Another way to say what this book is about is: what makes you tick and what ticks you off? We are all wired differently; however, common patterns of behavior can be noticed, defined, and studied.

There's an old adage that says, "You are the sum total of your experiences—whether they be good or bad." However, when you take your experiences and mesh them with your personality, you really have a better picture of what makes you tick. Your actions and reactions can be categorized into four basic types of personality behavior. The focus of this book will be to help you identify which of the four primary types of personality behavior you exhibit and how the four types interact together.

In addition to bringing understanding about yourself, this information will absolutely revolutionize how you relate to your spouse, children, co-workers, boss, and even your pastor.

Many times relationships are strained because of personality conflicts. We often spend much of our lives "walking on eggshells" around certain people just to avoid these conflicts.

Rather than spending that time avoiding a particularly annoying personality-type, spend some time reading this book and learning how to relate and interrelate with these personalities. The product of your learning about the four basic types of personalities will greatly enhance your communication skills. With this information, you will be able to identify and relate to others around you with more clarity and effectiveness.

Most conflict is primarily the result of a miscommunication and misunderstanding. Frustration is the product of un-met expectations; we expect people to act in a certain way, but they do not. As you grow in understanding of the four basic personality types, conflict and frustration will be greatly reduced in your life and can become extinct.

When a person prepares for a career, years of study and preparation usually precede launching into that career. It has always amazed me that we will spend years of study for a temporal thing like a career, but we rarely spend time studying and developing ways to communicate and interrelate with people. This is especially true regarding relationships with our spouses and children.

Many divorce courts would be emptied if people spent a few hours studying about what makes people tick and what ticks them off. I challenge you to spend time in this book and put into practice the truths revealed in it. The results will be phenomenal! Let's begin this journey together...

WELCOME ABOARD!

2

WHY AM I THIS WAY?

I will praise You, for I am fearfully and wonderfully made; Marvelous are Your works, And that my soul knows very well (Psalm 139:14).

Why am I this way? How many times has this question been asked through the years of man's existence? You are not the first person to ask it nor will you be the last. However, I have good news. In the eyes of the Creator, you have been wonderfully and fearfully made and ALL of His works are marvelous! That includes you.

Some will ask, "What went wrong?" It is not so much that something has gone wrong as it is that something has not been completed.

Building a Pool

Suppose you were going to build a swimming pool. There is much planning, time, and resources that go into the building of a pool. There is also much anticipation of the use of the pool especially when summer is just around the corner.

However, until that pool gets "completed" it is just a hole in the earth. When it rains, it gets muddy and dangerous. You look outside at your once beautiful back yard, and it looks like giant moles have been partying for a long time at your expense. Not only is there a big hole in the ground, but there are mounds of dirt piled up on every side. You cannot have any backyard cookouts and the kids can no longer play outside.

Suddenly, all of that energy and excitement about building a pool is now replaced with frustration and discontentment. Everyone is unhappy. The source of the problem and conflict is not that a pool is being built; it is that the pool has not been completed. It has not been finished; it is still in the rough.

However, once the pool is completed and finished, the time for energy and excitement returns. The family is now happy to have the pool. Friends and neighbors are invited over and life is good again.

Refining you personality is a lot like building a pool. There has to be time and planning spent on the front end learning about what to do and how it needs to be done. Many times, "rough" personalities are just unfinished.

The Lord has given to us the basic building blocks of personality traits but we are tasked with the responsibility of "finishing" and completing these traits. The goal of this book is to help you refine and put a finish on those traits.

The first thing that has to be understood is that no one has a "bad" personality. There is no such thing as a bad personality. Remember, you are fearfully and wonderfully made by a God who does not make mistakes. You are not an accident or an afterthought. You have been fearfully and wonderfully made by an almighty Creator for an almighty purpose.

God did not look down from Heaven and wonder what to do with you. He has a plan and a purpose for your life and it is good!

> For I know the thoughts that I think toward you, says the LORD, thoughts of peace and not of evil, to give you a future and a hope. Then you will call upon Me and go and pray to Me, and I will listen to you. And you will seek Me and find Me, when you search for Me with all your heart (Jeremiah 29:11-13).

The Lord God has good thoughts about you and your life. He knows the plan for your life and He has already started equipping you for the completion of that plan. The first layer of equipping is your personality. Many times we struggle over the plan and purpose that God has for our lives because we have not developed or completed the building or understanding the first tools He provided to us.

Personality development actually begins at conception and finishes at death. The goal is to have a process of continuous improvement working to develop and improve on one of the first tools that the Lord has given us to help fulfill His plan and purpose.

Looking to the Eternal

Your personality is a gift given by a loving and caring Father because you will need that gift in order to work and fulfill your part of His plan! In the midst of living our lives, the Lord wants us to be molded and shaped into His image. It is God's desire for you to succeed in every area of your life.

The true measure of success is not how high you can climb on the corporate ladder as much as it is ensuring that the ladder is against the correct wall. Can you imagine spending years climbing the corporate ladder only to get to the top and discover that the ladder is against the wrong building? Many people are working to climb a temporal ladder of business success only to lose the eternal parts of their lives such as their spouses, children, and even their own souls.

No one on their deathbed ever wishes that they had spent more time at the office or on closing one more deal for the boss.

We need to learn to measure the success of our lives in terms of eternity rather than in terms of the temporary.

Businesses will come and go. Today we find many that were once large, strong corporations no longer in business. Some of the most powerful and influential people are no longer in this world. Some have even found themselves in prison. No one sets out on a course in life with the goal of making it into the prison system or a divorce court; many find themselves in places they never expected.

You're Equipped With Good Gifts

One of the greatest tools for success in life, business, and marriage is the original gift that the Lord has already given to you—your personality! You have been given your personality because that is the one that you need in order to do what you are supposed to do!

NEVER consider that your personality is bad. Unfinished, maybe. Incomplete, possibly. Rough around the edges, probably. But bad? NEVER! God does NOT give "bad" gifts.

All of His gifts are given ON purpose FOR a purpose.

ARE THERE OTHERS OUT THERE LIKE ME?

And you, fathers, do not provoke your children to wrath, but bring them up in the training and admonition of the Lord (Ephesians 6:4).

You are not alone and God has not left you without help and support. Not only are there others out there like you, but many of them are very successful in life. One of the keys to a successful life is to release your personality into the plan and purpose reserved for you by the Creator of all things. The plan and purpose for your life is just one of the things that He has created for you.

The plan and purpose the Lord has for your life is not hidden from you, but it is hidden for you! The key to unlocking success in that plan is to release your personality into it which means do not spend time trying to change your personality because the change may not unlock your destiny. It's not time to be like someone else.

At the same time, do not use your personality as an excuse for your behavior. Your personality is not an excuse. It is a tool to be honed, developed, and released. When we try to use it as an excuse for our behavior, we are absolving ourselves of the requirement to grow in the admonition of the Lord. Ephesians 6:1-4 says:

> *Children, obey your parents in the Lord, for this is right. "Honor your father and mother," which is the first commandment with promise: "that it may be well with you and you may live long on the earth." And you, fathers, do not provoke your children to wrath, but bring them up in the training and admonition of the Lord.*

Growing Forward

The natural development of a child is toward growth. The change your child encounters becomes a product of time for their spirit, soul, and body. Many parents desire to keep their children young to protect them from the things of the world; however, time passes and children grow and develop. You just can't stop it.

The same is true of our personalities. Time comes and goes at a constant rate. Just as it is impossible to stop a healthy child from growing, so it is impossible to stop a personality from growing and developing—you just need to guide it in the right direction.

A successful person will grow and develop the strengths of their personality rather than simply allowing them to develop on its own. Fate and circumstance are not good producers of personalities. Only the One who created your personality can help you grow and understand it.

Building a Strong Team

One key to successful leadership is to strengthen your strengths and staff your weaknesses. Some will say that it is best to work on and strengthen your weaknesses. This is simply misdirection in leadership and success. You should improve your weaknesses, but why spend time, resources, and energy on employing something that is weak? The goal of success in leadership is to develop a team around you to accomplish the task—using the best of everyone's gifts. No one is an independent or self-sufficient island unto themselves.

It is commonly said that there is no "I" in team. There is also no "I" in success. However, there is a "u" and an "s" to make "us." Success and successful leadership are the products of building a team to go forth and change the world. To be a successful team member, each person needs to develop and allow their personality to grow.

Be an Original

When people are forming a team, the natural tendency is to surround themselves with people who are like-minded. We are naturally more comfortable with people who are just like us. Opposites often attract, but perhaps that is why spouses spend much of their time trying to get the other person to be perfect—just like them! Besides, if your spouse was perfect they would not need you!

However, the essence of team building and forming a team is NOT to surround yourself with more people like yourself, but to find people who are different in order to use their strengths instead of your weaknesses. If a person only looks to find a duplicate, then one of them is not needed! Noted author John Mason says that you are born an original, do not die a copy. Strength is created in a piece of rope when different and various strands are woven together. If you want to build a strong team, then different and various personalities have to be woven together, but it takes skill to do that. The wisdom of King Solomon is recorded in Ecclesiastes 3:9-12:

> *Two are better than one, because they have a good reward for their labor. For if they fall, one will lift up his companion. But woe to him who is alone when he falls, for he has no one to help him up. Again, if two lie down together, they will keep warm; but how can one be warm alone? Though one may be overpowered by another, two can withstand him. And a threefold cord is not quickly broken.*

The Scriptural truth is that a three-fold cord is not easily broken. The challenge becomes to know what cords to weave together. Resist the tendency to surround yourself with duplicates or copies. Instead, begin to bring others to the team who are different from you. There is strength in that diversity. God has created you with a built-in interdependency on these others.

While there are others in the world with your same personality type, strive to surround yourself with others NOT like you. Allow those around you to grow in the development and admonition of the Lord. Many of the answers that you are looking for are found in the other members of your team. However, those answers have to grow and develop as the personality of those people grow and develop.

If we spend all of our time trying to make those around us to be copies or duplicates, then we may miss the very solutions that the Lord has already provided in our path. That spouse who is the exact opposite of you may be the place where your solutions are hidden. Again, your God-given tools for success are not hidden from you, but for you.

Develop the team around you by looking for diverse people. Build that team to strengthen your weaknesses. As you release your strength into the team, the strengths of others will be released as well. THAT three-fold or even four-fold cord cannot and will not be easily broken.

The Big 4

"All men by nature desire knowledge."
—Aristotle

The goal of any leadership is the development of a team to work together in order to accomplish a task. This may be in a business, family, or in your relationships. It is the function of the leader to move that group from the unknown parts of the task to the known and accomplished parts of the task. While this may be easy to write on paper, the actual accomplishment of the task may be quite challenging. Effective leaders will "stack the deck" in their favor by selecting who gets to work on the team. This is where the initial challenge begins!

The most difficult part of accomplishing a task or goal is NOT the actual work involved. Nor is it merely the identification of the completed task or goal. The most difficult task is the one part that is often overlooked—building the TEAM.

Too many times, the membership of a team is simply who happens to be present at the time. Many leaders will simply survey the room, pick the people that they like (or are like them), and form the team, which is then sent out to accomplish the impossible—working together to develop a solution or accomplish a task.

Wouldn't it be great to have a reliable system to use in helping put together a winning team EVERY TIME? That is exactly what this book is about!

Just as "team" has four letters, the key to putting together a successful team has four letters: DISC. The DISC form of leadership is not a new concept. It has been around for many years.

As early as 400 BC, Aristotle, who built on the work of Hippocrates, noted that four basic elements of nature could be identified. He identified these as humors and tied them to personal behavioral patterns in people. Several hundred years later around 190 AD, a Greek physician named Galenus of Pergamum, who is better known as Galen, indentified four common temperaments. Galen named these four temperaments or personality patterns: choleric, sanguine, phlegmatic, and melancholy.

Cholerics can be characterized by the element of fire, the season of summer, and the color red, especially fiery red. He recognized cholerics as ambitious and driven, as well as easily angered and temperamental.

According to Galen, a sanguine is optimistic, fun-loving, popular, and talkative. Sanguines, many times, are characterized by the element of air, the season of spring and childhood, and the color sunny yellow.

Galen identified phlegmatics as a person who is calm and unemotional. Additionally, the phlegmatics were generally self-content and kind; their shy personality can often inhibit enthusiasm in others and make themselves seem lazy and resistant to change. They are very consistent, relaxed, and observant, making them good administrators and diplomats. Like the sanguine personality, the phlegmatic have many friends, but are more reliable and compassionate. Phlegmatics were most often associated with the element water, the color opaque, and the season of winter.

To Galen, the melancholics were stubborn and difficult to change. Yet, he found them to be very analytical and logical. Often very kind and considerate, melancholics can be highly creative—as in poets and artists—but can also become overly obsessed on the tragedy and cruelty in the world, thus becoming depressed. Their season is autumn; their element is earth; and their color is black. A melancholic is often a perfectionist, being very particular about what they want and how they want it in some cases. This often results in being dissatisfied with one's own artistic or creative works, always pointing out what could and should be improved in themselves and others.

In order to understand and categorize personalities, other studies have mapped four types of animals, four types of strategies, four types of attitudes, four types of character, four types of worldviews—even four types of thinking. Most studies agree in finding four specific types of behavior patterns. The DISC model is no different and builds upon the others.

The DISC model is an acronym for:

> Dominance
> Influence
> Steadiness
> Conscientiousness

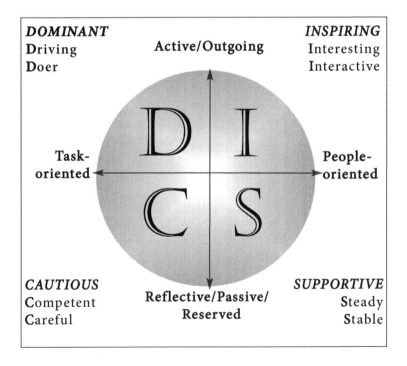

These four areas of human behavior closely correspond to Hippocrates' original description of humors. To illustrate the four types, they can be grouped in a grid with "D" and "I" sharing the top row and representing outgoing or extroverted aspects of a person's behavior, while the "C" and "S" represent a passive or introverted aspect. "D" and "C" represent task-focused aspects, and "I" and "S" represent social aspects. The simple matrix on the preceding page can better explain.

The original DISC Assessment Model was developed by John Geier and others and based on the 1928 work of psychologist William Moulton Marston PhD (1893–1947). DISC is the four quadrant behavioral model developed to examine the behavior of individuals in their environment or within a specific situation. It therefore focuses on the styles and preferences of such behavior. Marston graduated from doctoral studies at Harvard in the newly developing field of psychology and was also a consulting psychologist, researcher, and author or co-author of five books.

This system of dimensions of observable behavior has become known as the universal language of behavior. Research has found that characteristics of behavior can be grouped into these four major personality styles or expressions, and they tend to exhibit specific characteristics common to that particular style. All individuals will operate or express all four types of patterns, but what differs from one to another is the extent of each.

Most people will express or blend two of the four styles in varying degrees. According to Dr. Mels Carbonell, most types are seen in shades of grey rather than black or white, and within that, there is interplay of behaviors, otherwise known as blends. The denotation of such blends starts with the primary (or stronger) type, followed by the secondary (or lesser) type, although all contribute more than just purely the strength of that "signal."

Understanding the differences between these blends makes it possible to integrate individual team members with less troubleshooting. In a typical team, there are varying degrees of compatibility, not just toward tasks but interpersonal relationships as well. However, when they are identified, energy can be spent on refining the results.

Each personality type has its own unique value to the team, general characteristics, ideal environment, and the individual's motivation.

The word **DISC** has four letters and each letter represents a descriptive personality type.

> Dominance – relating to control, power, and assertiveness
> Influence – relating to social situations and communication
> Steadiness – relating to patience, persistence, and thoughtfulness
> Conscientiousness – relating to structure and organization

THE "D" PERSONALITY: DIRECT & DEMANDING

So, being sent out by the Holy Spirit, they [Paul and Barnabas] went down to Seleucia, and from there they sailed to Cyprus. And when they arrived in Salamis, they preached the word of God in the synagogues of the Jews (Acts 13:4-5).

The active "D" type personality is closely related to the Type "A" person. This personality can be demanding, direct, and dominating. In their mind, no challenge is too big and no obstacle is too hard to overcome. Persistence and determination are common traits for these people. They love a challenge and love to challenge anything and everything. For this person, the status quo only exists to be changed and re-created.

You can see in this quote from Acts 13 that Paul was active in going out and leading others to complete the plan and purpose that God had for him.

People who are high in their intensity of the "D" style are active in dealing with problems and challenges, while low "D's" are people who want to do more research before committing to a decision. High "D" people are described as demanding, forceful, egocentric, strong-willed, driving, determined, ambitious, aggressive, and pioneering. In contrast to that, people who score more as a **low "D"** are described as those who are conservative, low-key, cooperative, calculating, undemanding, cautious, mild, agreeable, modest, and peaceful.

High "D" personalities are people that change the world around them. They make great entrepreneurs as well as world class criminals. Statements such as, "My way or the highway" are commonplace. They are movers and doers.

This personality is active towards tasks. However, they don't specialize in task completion. These people will have ten ongoing tasks and will be ready to take on more. Their greatest challenge is to focus on completing a task prior to starting a new one. They are goal-oriented, but will seldom take the time to write things down. All of their plans exist in their head, not on paper. They like to "shoot from the hip" and ask questions later. They will ask for forgiveness after the fact, rather than permission up-front.

Hand these people a task and they will quickly start the process. While they are not always seen as a team player, their value to the team is to get things started and moving; they help overcome inertia. This personality does not like to work in a closely supervised environment as this will quench their ideas and actions.

A "D" type of personality does not have, use, or think they need any social interaction skills. For them, it is all about the tasks—not the people. They have a tendency to be explosive and afterwards take you to the best restaurant in town for lunch as if nothing ever happened. They are always moving forward. What happened in the past is behind them. Their mind is already on the future.

A "D" leader must realize that people are important, and tasks need to be completed. This type of person enjoys starting tasks and will easily have over 10 different projects going at once. Finishing projects or tasks is not one of their strong points. It is important to remember to focus on one task at a time and bring it to completion. The Apostle Paul was this type of leader, but realized that he must learn to focus on completing one thing at a time.

> Not that I have already attained, or am already perfected; but I press on, that I may lay hold of that for which Christ Jesus has also laid hold of me. Brethren, I do not count myself to have appre-

> hended; but one thing I do, forgetting those things which are behind and reaching forward to those things which are ahead, I press toward the goal for the prize of the upward call of God in Christ Jesus (Philippians 3:12-14).

As I said earlier, the importance of this personality to the team will be the ability to get things started and moving forward. If you are the leader of a "D" personality, they like options and freedom to let their creativity run wild. You do not have to worry about getting them started—just holding them back enough to avoid getting frustrated and moving on to the next thing before it's time.

"D's" must learn to come under authority and work within the established guidelines. They don't play well with others, and they do not like their decisions challenged. However, given the proper information and options, they will change a decision at a moment's notice. They believe that a decision is made to be changed, and the only purpose for a plan is to have something to change! They are spontaneous and work well under pressure. Actually, pressure simply becomes a catalyst to start more tasks.

Many times, they become the "go-to" person because of their ability to get things started.

This personality is hard-driving and hard-charging. They will often run over people to get the task started and to keep the task moving forward. Their greatest strength is also their greatest weakness. The strength of persistence and determination will cause a "D" personality to look, and perhaps become, arrogant and self-willed.

To guide your "D" personality towards maturity, it requires that you temper persistence with discipline and to match determination with empathy. It is important for you to be able to sincerely show care and compassion as you work with people. Remember, people are NOT tools for the "D" to use in completing a task, but those people are created in the image of God and are valuable and important to Him.

As a "D," when you work with people, make it your goal to help them accomplish the plan and purpose that God has for their life. As you work toward this goal, your purpose will be revealed. One of the greatest truths in the Bible is found in Galatians 6:6-8:

> Let him who is taught the word share in all good things with him who teaches. Do not be deceived, God is not mocked; for whatever a man sows, that he will also reap. For he who sows to his flesh will of the flesh reap corruption, but he who sows to the Spirit will of the Spirit reap everlasting life.

Sow purpose to others and you
will reap purpose in your life!

D

Dominant, Direct, Demanding, Doing & Driving

Active & Task-Oriented

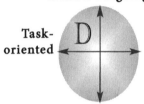

Greatest Strength:
    Getting a task started

Greatest Fear:
    Being embarrassed

Greatest Challenges:
    Not finishing tasks
    Submitting to authority

Bible Example:
    Paul

Need to focus on:
    The value of others
    Finishing Tasks

The "I" Personality: Inspiring & Influential

> But Peter, standing up with the eleven, raised his voice and said to them, "Men of Judea and all who dwell in Jerusalem, let this be known to you, and heed my words. For these are not drunk, as you suppose, since it is only the third hour of the day. But this is what was spoken by the prophet Joel" (Acts 2:14-16).

On the Day of Pentecost, Peter was the one who stood up and proclaimed the word of the Lord about the gift of the Holy Spirit. When Peter was active, he was always active towards people—not tasks.

In addition to the "D," the "I" personality is also very active. Whereas the "D" person is active toward tasks, this personality is active toward people. They are charismatic and can be charming and may come across as manipulating other people to get their way.

Have you ever seen the kid in class who raises their hand to answer a question, but when called on they have no idea of what the question even was? This is the untainted "I" personality. Their personality is energized by other people at whatever cost.

This personality seems to get very little accomplished, which is fine with them. They just want and need to be around people. They are not confrontational and are susceptible to peer-pressure.

Many times, they will go against their own convictions in order to "go with the crowd." Peer approval is important to them and sought after.

While there is no "I" in team, there is definitely the word "me," and that is the basis for this personality. It's all about "me." Anyone is welcome to come along on the journey, but just remember who the journey is about!

The "I" personality is the life of the party. This person will talk to anyone at the "drop of a hat" and will even drop the hat just to be able to talk. The "I" person never meets a stranger and you will leave a conversation thinking that you are their new best friend.

People with high "I" tendencies influence others through talking and activity and tend to be emotional. They are described as convincing, magnetic, political, enthusiastic, persuasive, warm, demonstrative, trusting, and optimistic.

For those with **low "I"** tendencies, they influence more by data and facts, and not with feelings. They are described as reflective, factual, calculating, skeptical, logical, suspicious, matter-of-fact, pessimistic, and critical.

For the high "I," attention to detail and follow-through is not important. Their charm and charisma can often lead them to take on many tasks, which may never actually get started—much less completed.

These people can become a strong leader through their natural ability to inspire. They also make great con men. An "I" is very spontaneous and thinks better "on their feet" than with a prepared speech.

When you are leading "I" personalities, remember that recognition and praise are important to these people. Also, remember that when you are talking, an "I" person is not really listening to you, but trying to figure out how to get back in control of the conversation. It may not be a conscious thought, but this is how that personality works. Instead of listening, they are thinking about what they want to say next.

Listening skills are NOT in their natural skill set; this needs to become a learned behavior. You may have to repeat yourself often, write it down for them, and then have the "I" relate back to you what you want them to do. They will remember every PERSON that you want them to meet, but NOT what you want them to talk about.

Because of their ability to be flexible and spontaneous, they can quickly turn a situation to their favor and come out of the situation looking very good. They respond to pressure by becoming even more talkative and persuasive.

To grow and mature, this person needs to temper inspiration with detail and must learn that others, besides themselves, have goals and influence. The "I" needs to remember: rather than looking toward yourself and what people can do for you, begin to look at other people and what you can do for them.

> *Therefore if there is any consolation in Christ, if any comfort of love, if any fellowship of the Spirit, if any affection and mercy, fulfill my joy by being likeminded, having the same love, being of one accord, of one mind. Let nothing be done through selfish ambition or conceit, but in lowliness of mind let each esteem others better than himself. Let each of you look out not only for his own interests, but also for the interests of others* (Philippians 2:1-4).

As great as you may count yourself, the "I" must learn to esteem others even higher. As you invest yourself in relationships that help others, you will find the greatest release for your inspiration and influence. As you grow and mature, you will shift away from what others can do for you, and begin to think about what you can do for them.

As you add task completion to your "I" personality skill set, you will develop into a strong and accomplished leader. The "I" has a natural ability to care for people, but not a natural ability to take care of tasks.

Inspiration and influence are two of the most powerful tools available to become a great leader. People skills are your specialty. You have a tremendous ability to draw crowds together and motivate them to a higher purpose.

As you submit these skills to God, He will bring others into your life that will push these skills to much higher levels. Your key to success is realizing that you need other people to pull on you to release your purpose in God.

I

Inspiring, Influential, Interesting & Interactive

Active & People-Oriented

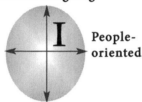

Greatest Strengths:
    Bring a group together
    Flexibility & spontaneity

Greatest Fear:
    Being overlooked

Greatest Challenge:
    Sharing the spotlight with others

Bible Example:
    Peter

Need to focus on:
    Organization
    Time management
    Listening

THE "S" PERSONALITY: STEADY & STABLE

> He [Andrew] first found his own brother Simon, and said to him, "We have found the Messiah" (John 1:41).

The "S" personality influences one-on-one to bring people together and works more efficiently and effectively behind the scenes. The Apostle Andrew is a perfect example.

> Again, the next day, John stood with two of his disciples. And looking at Jesus as He walked, he said, "Behold the Lamb of God!" The two disciples heard him speak, and they followed Jesus. Then Jesus turned, and seeing them following, said to them, "What do you seek?" They said to Him, "Rabbi" (which is to say, when translated, Teacher), "where are You staying?" He said to them, "Come and see." They came and saw where He

> was staying, and remained with Him that day (now it was about the tenth hour). One of the two who heard John speak, and followed Him, was Andrew, Simon Peter's brother. He first found his own brother Simon, and said to him, "We have found the Messiah" (which is translated, the Christ). And he brought him to Jesus (John 1:45-42).

The "S" personality is always on everybody's "get-to-know" list. They provide the stability and backbone for any and all groups or organizations. These people are literally the glue which hold everything together and are the easiest people to get along with and be around. They are the nicest people in the group and are just fun to be around.

While this personality is passive toward people, their value is immeasurable to the group. They may seem to be quiet and shy at first, but they REALLY warm up once they get to know you. They will talk very little in the beginning stages of the group; however, once they are comfortable with people, they can talk non-stop. "S" personalities are very easy to talk to and comfortable to be around.

They want to know "who" is involved prior to committing to a task, project, party, or dinner. They are the perfect balance to the look-at-me "I" personality because they prefer to talk to people behind the scenes. When the task or group runs into trouble spots, they calm everyone down and keep them focused and working together.

The "S" personality prefers people over tasks, but prefers to work one-on-one or in small groups. Many times the more active personalities, "D" and "I," will take the credit for much of the work done by the "S." However, that is fine with the "S;" they are not interested and would strongly prefer NOT to be in the limelight or get all the attention. Their quiet nature leads them to be thoughtful and intuitive people.

People with high "S" traits want a steady pace, security, and do not like sudden changes. High "S" individuals are calm, relaxed, patient, possessive, predictable, deliberate, stable, consistent, and tend to be unemotional or poker-faced. In contrast, **low "S"** intensity traits are those who like change and variety. People with low "S" tendencies are described as restless, impatient, demonstrative, eager, or impulsive.

The "S" personalities are not strong task-oriented people; their strength is in looking out for others. They are much more interested in the general welfare of the people in the group rather than actually getting the work done which becomes the need of this personality. To be successful, it is important for them to acknowledge the task while working to keep the group together.

To this personality group, it is all about their relationship to others. A wise leader will recognize this and "task" the "S" to work with the people of the group. Where the "I" is all about "me," the "S" is all about "you."

S

Steady, Stable & Supportive

Reflective/Passive/Reserved & People-Oriented

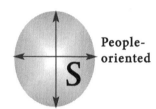

Greatest Strengths:
>   Backbone of a group
>   Working behind the scenes

Greatest Fear:
>   Being alone

Greatest Challenge:
>   Confrontation

Bible Example:
>   Andrew

Need to focus on:
>   Standing up for what they believe
>   Friendship isn't everything

THE "C" PERSONALITY: COMPETENT & COMPLIANT

And so it was, on the next day, that Moses sat to judge the people; and the people stood before Moses from morning until evening (Exodus 18:13).

Moses was the judge for the children of Israel. God's standards became his standards, and he was good at holding others accountable to those standards. He was compliant to God's standards. His personality was wired so that he could handle the monotony of hearing the same stories day in and day out.

Moses was a strong personality, but he never desired to be out front getting all the attention. Actually, if you remember, the Lord practically had to force him to go out in front and even promised to give him the words to speak.

The "C" personalities are truly the people who perform the actual work of a task or project.

While being passive or reflective towards tasks, the amount of work accomplished is many times staggering. They prefer a checklist of items to be accomplished. The leader of the group may have to help the "C" personality with the list, but once it has been developed they will work tirelessly and efficiently in completing the list.

This is where much of the actual work gets done. While the "S" provides the glue, the "C" provides the substance and task completion for the group. The "C" personalities are not strong in relationships, but they are very strong in task completion.

Most significant to the "C" traits is competency. Whereas, the "D" thinks they are always right, the "C" IS always right. It is best not to disagree too quickly with a "C" because you will most likely be apologizing soon!

"C" types are slow in making a decision, but once the decision is made it is virtually immutable. "C" personalities make great analysts. They will analyze something from every known angle and will even make up angles to study. This gives the appearance of being slow to decide, but to them all the facts are valuable and must be considered prior to making an accurate and lasting conclusion.

People with high "C" styles adhere to rules, regulations, and structure. These people are good in quality control and compliance review. They like to do quality work and do it right the first time.

A "C" personality is known for being compliant which can by definition be seen as obedient, submissive, or yielding; however, this is not the "C" personality. It's important to understand that this personality is compliant, but it's being compliant to their own personal standards. If their standards differ from the company rules, it will be their standards that they follow. The goal for a "C" should be to make God's standards their own.

The "C" personality has built-in the ability to follow Shakespeare's admonition: "to thine own self be true"—regardless of circumstance or outside pressure. This is the single person in a jury who votes innocent when everyone else votes guilty; if they change their mind, it will be because they are absolutely convinced that they are wrong—not pressured into it.

High "C" people are careful, cautious, exacting, neat, systematic, diplomatic, accurate, and tactful.

Those with **low "C"** scores challenge the rules and want independence and are described as self-willed, stubborn, opinionated, arbitrary, unsystematic, and unconcerned with details.

C

COMPETENT, COMPLIANT & CAUTIOUS

REFLECTIVE/PASSIVE/RESERVED & TASK-ORIENTED

Greatest Strengths:
    Accuracy
    Quality control

Greatest Fear:
    Being wrong

Greatest Challenges:
    Flexibility
    Taking risks

Bible Examples:
    Moses & Thomas

Need to focus on:
    Avoiding perfectionism
    Trust & faith

PUT IT IN THE BLENDER

> *And we know that all things work together for good to those who love God, to those who are the called according to His purpose* (Romans 8:28).

When you put personalities in the blender, the mix that it produces is good for the purposes of God. People will be strong in some of these traits and weaker in others. You may be reading this and think that some characteristics apply to you from two or even three of the personality types.

The vast majority of people will develop and display blends of the four types. The blends can also change based on a particular circumstance. When discovering your personality type, it's important to take a specific environment into consideration. At work, you may be in charge and behave as a "D" personality; however, at home you might be the life of the party as an "I." Most people are stronger in one type, but will also have many traits of another type. The goal is to be balanced in all four types.

Many times, the interaction of these traits will manifest differently from one person to another. This explains why two people with the same personality type will still be somewhat different. The intensities and percentages of the traits will vary with each individual—at the same time, a person's circumstance and maturity will also impact the various personality traits.

> *For You formed my inward parts; You covered me in my mother's womb. I will praise You, for I am fearfully and wonderfully made; Marvelous are Your works, And that my soul knows very well. My frame was not hidden from You, When I was made in secret, And skillfully wrought in the lowest parts of the earth* (Psalm 139:13-15).

Scripture declares that each individual person is fearfully and wonderfully made. You are a unique creation formed and created by a unique God for a unique purpose. You were created on purpose for a specific purpose.

It is important to be yourself. As bestseller author John Mason would say, "You are born an original; don't die a copy." While there may be no one else exactly like you, there are many people with similar traits. These similarities produce patterns that can be recognized.

We all go into the blender with our different intensities and percentages of our personality traits. What comes out makes each one of us unique in the eyes of the Lord and better prepared for the purpose and destiny that He has called us to complete.

God is good all the time and all the time God is good! He only has good things in store for His people. There is only goodness in God. You are made in His image. This means that you have the goodness of God inside you!

All that He is will be poured out into His children. So when we come out of the blender of personality types, we come out better equipped for the plan and purpose that He has for us!

The "D" Blends

For example, it is common for a "D" personality to also have a mixture of the "I" personality. The result is a task-driven active person who also enjoys being with people. This person will not HAVE to be the "life of the party," but will enjoy being a part of the party. Both types are active, but the intensities and percentages will determine if they are more people or task-oriented.

The "other" side of the "DI" personality can come across as a Drill Instructor: fully task-oriented and gets everyone doing the task.

Whereas a "D" mixed with an "S" becomes task-oriented, but somewhat shy around people at first. However, they will soon warm up and get people involved doing something.

A "D" with some "C" mixed in becomes a person that is totally task-oriented. The challenge with this person is that the active part of the task personality needs to get something going, but the reflective—or passive—side needs to analyze each option. Many times it will seem that for every two steps forward one step is taken back.

The "I" Blends

The "I" personality can be a lot of fun when put into the blender. Remember, this personality is active toward people and never meets a stranger.

When an "I" personality is mixed with a "D" you get a person that is active toward tasks and people. However, the emphasis is a little more towards the people so it becomes easy for others to get involved with the task. Unlike the Drill Instructor type we saw above, this "ID" type is easier to follow and be around.

However, mixing an "I" with an "S" produces someone who is VERY oriented towards people. Don't assign them a lot of tasks without assigning them a lot of people.

The "IC" type is one of the more rare blends. Active people with strong analysis and detail skills are uncommon, yet valuable. They love to be around people and enjoy getting things done.

"S" Combinations

The "S" blender produces some interesting combinations. The "S" is somewhat shy, but very stable.

"SI" people are easy to get along with and fun to be around. They are not the life of the party, but they definitely want to know who is at the party. Often before an "S" commits to an event, they want to know who is going to be there; who is in attendance or involved will influence their decisions.

The "SC" blend is the most common for the "S" personality. Being reserved towards people and tasks can sometimes be challenging. They like clear direction and sincere motives.

The more rare combination of an "S" is when it is mixed with a "D." An "SD" person will be quietly accomplishing more than most other people. Their accomplishments may go unnoticed, but will accumulate quickly.

Mixing It Up With a "C"

Just like an "SC" is the most common for an "S" person, a "CS" is the most common blend for someone who is predominately a "C." The "CS" person is more task and checklist oriented, but has strong personal relationships with a few people. This is one of my favorite blends because my wife and daughter are "CS's!"

The "CD" blend is a task accomplishing machine. They love working from a checklist and will work until all things are checked off; they will not relent and will never give up.

Just as an "IC" blend is uncommon, so is the "CI." A task-oriented person who also enjoys being in a group is a rarity. Find them and keep them!

The personality blends add interesting flavor to a person's life and to a team. As you observe yourself in various situations, you will be able to discern both your primary and secondary traits.

I Am As God Has Made Me

Before I formed you in the womb I knew you (Jeremiah 1:5).

God knows each of us better than anyone else does, and He gave us our personalities. One of my favorite Scriptures in the Bible is Jeremiah 29:11:

For I know the thoughts that I think toward you, says the LORD, thoughts of peace and not of evil, to give you a future and a hope.

It is comforting to understand and realize that God has a hope and future for all of us. I especially like the Holman Christian Standard Bible translation of Jeremiah 29:11 using the word "plans":

"For I know the plans I have for you"— this is the LORD's declaration—"plans for your welfare, not for disaster, to give you a future and a hope."

The Lord of all creation has already declared that you have a future and a hope! God knows what He wants done through our lives; He is ever working on our behalf for good. Remember, God is good—all the time.

In His infinite goodness, He has a plan, purpose, and destiny that is unique to each of the billions of people alive today. Think about it: He has billions of people and billions of unique plans. Only the infinite mind from an infinite Creator can do this.

Mankind is not on earth by chance; we did not evolve from primordial ooze that leaked out of a chaotic environment. We are fearfully and wonderfully made by a great and wonderful Creator to accomplish great and wonderful things.

Just like we want our kids to be successful in life, imagine how much more our heavenly Father wants His kids to be successful in life. Just think if parents had the ability to give gifts to their children that would be vital to their success. Every parent would immediately and willingly provide those gifts and talents to enable success for their kids. How much more does God want and desire this for His kids? God wants to do exceedingly abundantly beyond anything that we can ask, think, or imagine!

While similarities in personalities exist, the truth of the matter is that each person has a unique, God-provided personality. The intensity levels will vary as well as the blending levels. The blends will make each personality expression different and unique.

Why Is This?

With over six billion people in the world and over six billion unique plans for their lives, each personality blend and expression must be unique. The Lord does not need copies or duplicates. He creates each and every one of us with a unique personality in order for us to fulfill the plan and purpose that He has for each and every life.

Every one of the unique plans given by the Lord requires a unique personality combination. God has made you the way that you are for a purpose. That purpose is to complete the plan that He has for you!

Many times, people will see someone else and want to be like them. The problem with that is that the other person was not called to do what you are called to do. Their purpose and destiny is different from yours, so the Lord has given you a different and distinct personality to complete what He has planned for your life.

Since the Lord knew you before you were in the womb, your personality is one of the first gifts given to you by Him. He knows the plans that He has for you and they are good. Therefore, the personality that He gave you is good because it is needed to complete the plan!

Let's look at Bible examples of the personality types. As we examine the actions, conversations, and relationships of these men of God, we can see how God used their personalities and how they matured with the help of the Holy Spirit. We will look at these men in context of Scripture and in light of history.

> Since God is good,
> He ONLY gives good gifts!

11

THE APOSTLE PAUL: DEMANDING, DECISIVE, & DOING

> As for Saul, he made havoc of the church, entering every house, and dragging off men and women, committing them to prison (Acts 8:3).

While the intensities and the blends of personalities will be unique, patterns do exist. These patterns not only exist today, but they also existed in Bible times.

Saul of Tarsus, the "D" personality that we will explore, is first introduced to Bible readers in Acts 7:58 at the stoning of the first Christian martyr, Stephen. Let me set the stage of how this Saul, with his active personality, set about doing his best to eliminate Christianity at its birth.

> When they heard these things they were cut to the heart, and they gnashed at him [Stephen] with their teeth. But he,

> being full of the Holy Spirit, gazed into heaven and saw the glory of God, and Jesus standing at the right hand of God, and said, "Look! I see the heavens opened and the Son of Man standing at the right hand of God!" Then they cried out with a loud voice, stopped their ears, and ran at him with one accord; and they cast him out of the city and stoned him. And the witnesses laid down their clothes at the feet of a young man named Saul. And they stoned Stephen as he was calling on God and saying, "Lord Jesus, receive my spirit." Then he knelt down and cried out with a loud voice, "Lord, do not charge them with this sin." And when he had said this, he fell asleep (Acts 7:54-60).

Saul is identified as a young man in verse 58. History records that Saul was born around 10-15 AD. This would put Saul in his late teens to early twenties at the time of this passage. Under normal circumstances, a young man would travel to Jerusalem around the age of 13, and we know that Saul studied under the renowned Rabban Gamaliel, who was the grandson of one of the most important figures in Jewish history, Hillel.

Saul was a member of the Sanhedrin, the Jewish ruling assembly, at the time. He was an ambitious, determined man who studied under the best, and he achieved success early and often. After the stoning of Stephen, Saul decisively went

The Apostle Paul: Demanding, Decisive, & Doing

on a one-man crusade to eradicate the religion of Jesus Christ.

The Bible goes on to elaborate about the stoning of Stephen and Saul's role to participate in the first persecution of the church in Acts chapter 8:

> Now Saul was consenting to his [Stephen's] death. At that time a great persecution arose against the church which was at Jerusalem; and they were all scattered throughout the regions of Judea and Samaria, except the apostles. And devout men carried Stephen to his burial, and made great lamentation over him. As for Saul, he made havoc of the church, entering every house, and dragging off men and women, committing them to prison (Acts 8:1-3).

We go on to see Saul's determination in Acts 9:1 where Saul is "breathing threats and murder against the disciples of Christ." At this point, Saul can be identified as an active, task-oriented leader with the goal of removing the Christian church from the face of the earth.

However, on his way to Damascus, he has an encounter that changes his life and future forever. Rules in dealing with a "D" personality: look them in the eyes and speak loudly. In Acts 9:3-6, we see how the Lord got Saul's attention in a dramatic encounter:

> *As he [Saul] journeyed he came near Damascus, and suddenly a light shone around him from heaven. Then he fell to the ground, and heard a voice saying to him, "Saul, Saul, why are you persecuting Me?" and he said, "Who are You, Lord?" Then the Lord said, "I am Jesus, whom you are persecuting. It is hard for you to kick against the goads." So he, trembling and astonished, said, "Lord, what do You want me to do?" Then the Lord said to him, "Arise and go into the city, and you will be told what you must do."*

At that moment, Saul's outlook and future changed, but the only thing that did not change was Saul's personality. After his conversion and subsequent healing from blindness at the hands of Ananias, Saul immediately began to preach Jesus Christ in the synagogues of Damascus.

After this conversion, he began the task of actively spreading the gospel around the known world. Saul of Tarsus became the Apostle Paul who traveled to more countries on foot than many today reach even with all the current modes of transportation available. Paul was determined to fulfill the Great Commission of going into the entire world and making Christian disciples all on his own.

Saul of Tarsus was direct, demanding, decisive, and doing all the wrong things. When he was converted to Christianity, his personality style did not change, only his purpose. The Apostle Paul continued to be direct, demanding, decisive, and doing the unique plan and purpose which he was called to complete. Paul spent the next 30 years of his life actively pursuing the task of expanding the Kingdom of God and was eventually beheaded by Nero and sent to Heaven to receive his reward. His personality style was uniquely suited for the plan and purpose that God called him to complete.

According to the renowned scholar Bernard Bass who is the author of the book entitled, **The Bass Handbook of Leadership**, task-oriented leaders like Paul are identified as achievement-oriented, production-oriented, goal achieving, and performance planning. In the landmark book, **Leadership in Organizations**, Gary Yukl proposes five purposes of task-oriented leader behavior:

(1) To PROPOSE an objective, introduce a procedure, present an agenda, and redirect attention to the task.
(2) To STIMULATE communication, seek specific information, or encourage the introduction of new ideas.
(3) To CLARIFY communication, reduce confusion, ask for interpretations, and show how different ideas are related.
(4) To SUMMARIZE accomplishments, to review or ask for reviews.
(5) To TEST for consensus about objectives, interpretations, evaluations, and readiness for decisions.

The Apostle Paul is a great example of the "D" personality—with all its strength and weaknesses. We would do well to remember that when we are converted or born again, our personality does not change—only its purpose!

12

THE APOSTLE PETER: IMPRESSIVE & INSPIRING

> *Simon Peter answered and said, "You are the Christ, the Son of the living God"* (Matthew 16:16).

Another apostle named Peter was also called by the Lord to accomplish great things in the Kingdom of God. In the Scripture, we see that his personality is much different from Paul's.

Let's look at the first time Peter is introduced to Bible readers in Matthew 4:18 where, along with his brother Andrew, he is identified as being a fisherman:

> *And Jesus, walking by the Sea of Galilee, saw two brothers, Simon called Peter, and Andrew his brother, casting a net into the sea; for they were fishermen. Then He said to them, "Follow Me, and I*

> will make you fishers of men." They immediately left their nets and followed Him (Matthew 4:18-20).

Peter and his brother, Andrew, grew up in Bethsaida, which means "house of fishing," which is located along the coast of Galilee. He has a vastly different upbringing than Saul of Tarsus. Peter has a different personality style and a different purpose in the Kingdom.

It was impulsive Peter who was called out of the boat to walk on the water, and He responded without a thought:

> Now in the fourth watch of the night Jesus went to them, walking on the sea. And when the disciples saw Him walking on the sea, they were troubled, saying, "It is a ghost!" And they cried out for fear. But immediately Jesus spoke to them, saying, "Be of good cheer! It is I; do not be afraid." And Peter answered Him and said, "Lord, if it is You, command me to come to You on the water." So He said, "Come." And when Peter had come down out of the boat, he walked on the water to go to Jesus (Matthew 14:27-30).

Peter is also the one who rashly rebuked Jesus in Matthew 16:22 when Jesus revealed the plan of God that He came to fulfill:

> From that time Jesus began to show to His disciples that He must go to Jerusalem, and suffer many things from the elders and chief priests and scribes, and be killed, and be raised the third day. Then Peter took Him aside and began to rebuke Him, saying, "Far be it from You, Lord; this shall not happen to You!" But He turned and said to Peter, "Get behind Me, Satan! You are an offense to Me, for you are not mindful of the things of God, but the things of men" (Matthew 16:21-24).

It was Peter who also succumbed to peer pressure and denied Jesus three times. He openly expressed his thoughts and was usually the first disciple to speak in any given situation.

God used Peter's personality on the Day of Pentecost when he was emboldened by the infilling of the Holy Spirit and preached the first sermon to the crowds where over 3000 people were born again (Acts 2:14-41).

Even though the Apostle John is with Peter in Acts chapter three, it is Peter who spontaneously responds to the man begging for alms:

> Who, seeing Peter and John about to go into the temple, asked for alms. And fixing his eyes on him, with John, Peter said, "Look at us." So he gave them his attention, expecting to receive some-

> *thing from them. Then Peter said, "Silver and gold I do not have, but what I do have I give you: In the name of Jesus Christ of Nazareth, rise up and walk." And he took him by the right hand and lifted him up, and immediately his feet and ankle bones received strength* (Acts 3:3-7).

This is the first recorded miracle performed by any of the apostles after the Day of Pentecost. Peter went on to preach in Solomon's Portico and was subsequently arrested. When he testified to the Sanhedrin, Peter was the one who boldly proclaimed that Jesus had been raised from the dead and that salvation was only available through Him (Acts 4:1-12).

In Acts chapter five, Peter and the other apostles were arrested once again. Yet, Peter was the one identified in Scripture as giving a response to the Sanhedrin council. Peter became the spokesman for the group and didn't mind being the focus of everyone's attention:

> *And when they had brought them, they set them before the council. And the high priest asked them, saying, "Did we not strictly command you not to teach in this name? And look, you have filled Jerusalem with your doctrine, and intend to bring this Man's blood on us!" But Peter and the other apostles answered and said: "We ought to obey God*

rather than men. The God of our fathers raised up Jesus whom you murdered by hanging on a tree. Him God has exalted to His right hand to be Prince and Savior, to give repentance to Israel and forgiveness of sins. And we are His witnesses to these things, and so also is the Holy Spirit whom God has given to those who obey Him" (Acts 5:27-32).

As a sidebar, it's interesting to note that while Scripture does not explicitly record that Saul of Tarsus was present here; he was a member of the Sanhedrin in Jerusalem and should have had full knowledge of the events of the day. Jesus was also brought to this same Sanhedrin in Matthew 26:57-68, which possibly suggests that Saul of Tarsus was present during the "trial" and execution of Jesus.

Even Paul's teacher, Rabban Gamaliel, started to be swayed by the influential Peter and the other apostles as recorded in Acts 5:33-40:

When they heard this, they were furious and plotted to kill them. Then one in the council stood up, a Pharisee named Gamaliel, a teacher of the law held in respect by all the people, and commanded them to put the apostles outside for a little while. And he said to them: "Men of Israel, take heed to yourselves what you intend to do regarding these men. For some time ago Theudas rose up, claim-

> *ing to be somebody. A number of men, about four hundred, joined him. He was slain, and all who obeyed him were scattered and came to nothing. After this man, Judas of Galilee rose up in the days of the census, and drew away many people after him. He also perished, and all who obeyed him were dispersed. And now I say to you, keep away from these men and let them alone; for if this plan or this work is of men, it will come to nothing; but if it is of God, you cannot overthrow it — lest you even be found to fight against God." And they agreed with him.*

These factors may be at the root of why Saul of Tarsus had such a strong response against the Christian faith prior to his conversion.

Now, back to our subject. Peter—who is always mindful of people—becomes the first apostle to reach out to the Gentiles because of his vision on the rooftop in Joppa which resulted in his visit to Cornelius, a centurion of the Italian Regiment in Acts chapter 10. However, this is not Peter's first encounter with a Roman soldier. He was in the Garden of Gethsemane when Judas came with troops to arrest Jesus. Where Peter reached for a sword and cut off the ear of Malchus in the Garden, the more mature and balanced Peter responds very differently to Cornelius by preaching the gospel of Jesus to him and his household.

> While Peter was still speaking these words, the Holy Spirit fell upon all those who heard the word. And those of the circumcision who believed were astonished, as many as came with Peter, because the gift of the Holy Spirit had been poured out on the Gentiles also (Acts 10:44-45).

Once again, it is Peter who responds to the people, and then the Holy Spirit is poured out to the Gentiles. He was also in Antioch with Paul ministering to the Gentiles until certain Jewish leaders came to the area. Being a leader that is motivated to please people, Peter withdrew from the Gentiles and was sharply rebuked by Paul for doing it in Galatians 2:11-14.

> Now when Peter had come to Antioch, I [Paul] withstood him to his face, because he was to be blamed; for before certain men came from James, he would eat with the Gentiles; but when they came, he withdrew and separated himself, fearing those who were of the circumcision. And the rest of the Jews also played the hypocrite with him, so that even Barnabas was carried away with their hypocrisy. But when I saw that they were not straightforward about the truth of the gospel, I said to Peter before them all, "If you, being a Jew, live in the manner of Gentiles and not as the Jews, why do you compel Gentiles to live as Jews? (Galatians 2:11-14).

Peter was a leader that was impulsive yet warm, friendly, outspoken, and active towards people. Like Paul, Peter continued to preach the gospel of Jesus Christ for about 30 years and is eventually crucified by Nero in Rome on an upside down cross. The beautiful Papal Basilica of Saint Peter in Rome has the remains of Peter laid to rest in the Tombs of the Popes and can be visited today.

It is of interest to note, that Nero and many other Roman leaders tried to extinguish the light of Christianity in a dark world. However, the great Roman Coliseum, which was recognized as the crucible of Roman rule, is in ruins today in Rome, while the Basilica of St. Peter is living and vibrant in Vatican City near Rome. It's also worthy to note with some vindication that inside the Coliseum ruins where so many Christians were slaughtered there now stands a huge cross.

Where Paul was more task-oriented, Peter is more people-oriented. Peter is concerned with what people think about him. Peter follows what is described as a relations-oriented leadership style that expresses concern for people and attempts to reduce emotional conflict by harmonizing relations among others.

Peter presents a personality style that is inspiring, influencing, impressing, inducing, and active towards people. His basic motivation is recognition and approval. He fulfilled the purpose that the Lord had for Him by using the personality given to him by the Lord.

THE APOSTLE ANDREW: STEADY, STABLE, & SECURE

One of His disciples, Andrew, Simon Peter's brother, said to Him, "There is a lad here who has five barley loaves and two small fish" (John 6:9).

The name "Andrew" means manly and brave with valor. The New Testament states that Andrew was the brother of Simon Peter.

Both he and Peter were fishermen by trade; hence, Jesus called them to be His disciples by saying that He will make them "fishers of men." At the beginning of Jesus' public life, these brothers lived together in the same house in Capernaum. Mark 1:29 reads, "Now as soon as they had come out of the synagogue, they entered the house of Simon and Andrew, with James and John."

As brothers tend to be, the men were very different. Where Peter was loud, boisterous, and the life of the party as the "I" personality, Andrew was more quiet, steady, stable, and secure. Andrew was more of an "S" personality.

The Gospel of John states that Andrew was a disciple of John the Baptist, whose testimony first led him to follow Jesus.

> *Again, the next day, John stood with two of his disciples. And looking at Jesus as He walked, he said, "Behold the Lamb of God!" The two disciples heard him speak, and they followed Jesus...One of the two who heard John speak, and followed Him, was Andrew, Simon Peter's brother. He first found his own brother Simon, and said to him, "We have found the Messiah" (which is translated, the Christ). And he brought him to Jesus* (John 1:35-37, 40-42).

Andrew preferred a more one-on-one encounter. He at once recognized Jesus as the Messiah, and he hastened to introduce him to his brother, Peter. Andrew wasn't the one chosen to preach to the multitudes, but God used his personality to minister to one person at a time. Mother Teresa once said, "Help one person at a time and always start with the person nearest you." This adage is the mantra for the "S" personality.

As noted above on the occasion of the miraculous feeding of the five thousand, it was Andrew who knew about the lone boy in the crowd and said to Jesus in Acts 6:9-6 that, "There is a boy here who has five barley loaves and two fishes: but what are these among so many?"

While quiet by nature, Andrew was loyal and a close member of Jesus' inner council of friends. For example, a few days before Jesus' death, certain Greeks asked Philip if they might see Jesus. Philip referred the matter to Andrew as to one of greater clout. Andrew brought stability and authority to the group.

In the gospels, Andrew is referred to as being present for some important occasions as one of the disciples closely attached to Jesus. Andrew preferred small groups and left the larger audiences to Peter. He worked better in the background and, consequently, not much more information is mentioned about him in the Scriptures.

From what we generally know of the Apostles, we can extrapolate the details. As one of the Twelve, Andrew was allowed into Jesus' inner-circle; he was present at the Last Supper; beheld the risen Lord; witnessed the Ascension; shared in the graces and gifts of the first Pentecost; and helped, amid threats and persecution, to establish the Gospel in Palestine and other areas.

According to church history and tradition, he is considered the founder and first bishop of the Church of Byzantium (later Constantinople) in

AD 38. Early church leaders such as Eusebius and Origen state that Andrew preached in Asia Minor and in Scythia, along the Black Sea as far as the cities of Volga and Kiev.

Christian history in the Ukraine holds that the Apostle Andrew is said to have preached on the southern borders of modern-day Ukraine, along the Black Sea. Legend has it that he travelled up the Dnieper River and reached the future location of Kiev, where he erected a cross on the site where the St. Andrew's Church of Kiev currently stands, and he prophesied the foundation of a great Christian city.

Like his brother Peter, Andrew traveled and ministered for about 30 years and is martyred by crucifixion at the city of Patras in Greece. Church tradition describes Andrew as bound, not nailed, to a Latin cross of the kind on which Jesus is said to have been crucified. However, because he deemed himself unworthy to be crucified in the same manner as the Lord Jesus, Andrew requested to be crucified on a cross of the form called *Crux decussata* (X-shaped cross) now commonly known as a "Saint Andrew's Cross."

The Apostle Andrew did not die right away, but instead he was left to suffer for two days. True to his nature and his personality, church tradition records that he continued to preach the gospel of Jesus Christ bound to the cross until he finally died.

Tradition states that his martyrdom took place during the reign of Nero, on November 30, AD 60 and both the Latin and Greek churches keep that day as his feast.

Because of his travels, Andrew became the patron saint of Scotland, Ukraine, Russia, Romania, Patras in Greece, Amalfi in Italy, Luqa in Malta (where Paul was previously shipwrecked), and Esgueira in Portugal. He was also the patron saint of Prussia.

While quiet and steady in his personality, he fulfilled his plan and purpose of expanding the Kingdom of God and preaching the Gospel throughout many countries. I shared a bit about Andrew here because no one ever talks about him and his behind-the-scenes success of bringing people to the Lord in these regions.

Church tradition places the Apostle Andrews' remains in the Cathedral of Amalfi in Italy.

14

THE APOSTLE THOMAS: CAUTIOUS & COMPETENT

Thomas answered and said to Him, "My Lord and my God!" (John 20:28).

Thomas the Apostle, or Didymus (meaning "Twin") was also one of the twelve Apostles of Jesus. Thomas was born in or near Galilee. Through the Scripture, we see that he represents a classic "C" personality. However, Thomas gets a bad rap for being called the Doubting Apostle. Even today, people who are skeptical are called a "Doubting Thomas."

In Thomas' best known appearance in the New Testament, he doubts the resurrection of Jesus and demands to touch Jesus' wounds before being convinced. It is very important to note that Jesus did NOT correct or chastise Thomas for wanting this proof; He simply said, "Touch and feel." However, upon seeing and touching the wounds of Jesus he boldly proclaims, "My Lord and my God."

> *Now Thomas, called the Twin, one of the twelve, was not with them when Jesus came. The other disciples therefore said to him, "We have seen the Lord." So he said to them, "Unless I see in His hands the print of the nails, and put my finger into the print of the nails, and put my hand into His side, I will not believe." And after eight days His disciples were again inside, and Thomas with them. Jesus came, the doors being shut, and stood in the midst, and said, "Peace to you!" Then He said to Thomas, "Reach your finger here, and look at My hands; and reach your hand here, and put it into My side. Do not be unbelieving, but believing." And Thomas answered and said to Him, "My Lord and my God!" Jesus said to him, "Thomas, because you have seen Me, you have believed. Blessed are those who have not seen and yet have believed"* (John 20:24-29).

Jesus knew that Thomas' cautious personality required concrete proof and evidence of what had transpired. He also knew that once Thomas had the proof or evidence he needed, he would serve Him without hesitancy for the duration of his life.

A "C" personality has a natural desire to analyze and question everything BEFORE making a decision. This is something that the "D" and "I" personalities need desperately to learn. Additionally, once a "C's" mind in convinced, the decision becomes immutable or unchangeable. The decision becomes written in stone, which is demonstrated by Thomas' response to the concrete proof and evidence that Jesus provided: "My Lord and my God." At that point, Thomas was fully persuaded and fully devoted to serve Jesus.

Thomas also spoke up when Lazarus died and the apostles didn't want to go back to Judea, where Jesus' fellow Jews had attempted to stone Him to death. However, Thomas is fully convinced and says bravely in John 11:16, "Let us also go, that we may die with him."

As a typical "C" personality, Thomas always has questions to ask.

> *"Let not your heart be troubled; you believe in God, believe also in Me. In My Father's house are many mansions; if it were not so, I would have told you. I go to prepare a place for you. And if I go and prepare a place for you, I will come again and receive you to Myself; that where I am, there you may be also. And where I go you know, and the way you know." Thomas said to Him, "Lord, we do not know where You are going, and how can we know the way?" Jesus said to him, "I am the way, the truth, and the life. No one comes to the Father except through Me* (John 14:1-6).

We see Thomas' competent, compliant, and cautious personality as we read what he said and did as told in the Bible accounts. However, God used Thomas as perhaps the only original Apostle who went outside the Roman Empire to preach the Gospel of Jesus Christ. Once convinced of the resurrection, Thomas was unstoppable. He never wavered from his purpose, even to the point of death. He is also believed to have covered the largest area during the time of his ministry, which includes modern Persia and India.

The Apostle Thomas is traditionally believed to have sailed to India in 52 AD to spread the Christian faith in Kerala, India. He is supposed to have landed at the ancient port of Muziris, which became extinct in 1341 AD due to a massive flood which realigned the coasts near Kodungalloor. He then went to Palayoor (near present day Guruvayoor), which was a Hindu priestly community at that time. He left Palayoor in AD 52 for the southern part of what is now the Kerala State.

According to church tradition, Thomas was at first reluctant to accept this mission, but the Lord appeared to him in a night vision and said, "Fear not, Thomas. Go away to India and proclaim the Word, for my grace shall be with you." This response is classic for his "C" personality; he resisted at first and Jesus had to appear to him and instruct him—not rebuke him or correct him, but instruct him. Not being active toward tasks, Thomas again required specific instruction, which is provided by the Lord without question or hesitation.

Thomas evangelized throughout India and then crossed to the southeast coast of India where, after carrying out a second mission, he died near Madras. The tradition among Christians in India is that Thomas was speared to death around AD 53. He is often pictured holding a spear.

Trust Keeps the Team Together

> There is nothing more difficult to take in hand, more perilous to conduct, or more uncertain in its success, than to take the lead in the introduction of a new order of things.
> —Niccolo Machiavelli

Which came first, the chicken or the egg? This age-old question actually has a simple answer: the chicken. In Genesis 1:25, God created the chicken on day five. Additionally, there had to be someone there to care and nurture the egg before it could hatch successfully; hence, the chicken came first. Other than a good fricassee, what does this have to do with leadership and personalities?

Everyone is a leader in some capacity of their lives—whether you are a mom, coach, mentor, teacher, or supervisor you can benefit from sound team-building skills. Like the egg, without proper care and attention, members of the group or team will never be able to grow and mature to their full potential. Just as the egg has to trust the chicken for its care, so do individual members of a team have to develop trust in their leader.

Trust is a mutual benefit derived from a covenantal relationship. The leader and the team have to build a trust relationship. Trust and credibility work together in building a successful team.

Putting people first is a key strategy for successfully completing a task or a goal; therefore, the team which is made up of individuals from each of the four DISC personality types must form a bond of trust. Higher trust levels build stronger ties in the group. Trust is a value that should transcend cultures and build stronger relationships between different personality styles.

"Style" is a small word with a lot of meaning. According to the online Merriam Webster dictionary, "style" can be a noun, verb, adjective, or adverb and has the basic definition which says, "a particular manner or technique by which something is done, created, or performed." Replacing the word "something" in this definition with the word "leadership" would produce a definition of leadership style as: a particular manner or technique by which leadership is done, created, or performed. That particular manner or technique is personality.

Regent University Professors Dr. Bruce Winston and Dr. Kathleen Patterson have provided the field of leadership with an integrated definition when they concluded:

> A leader is one or more people who selects, equips, trains, and influences one or more followers who have diverse gifts, abilities, and skills and focuses the followers to the organization's mission and objectives causing the followers to willingly and enthusiastically expend spiritual, emotional, and physical energy in a concerted coordinated effort to achieve the organizational mission and objectives.

Leadership and personality style become how that particular leader accomplishes this definition. Leadership is a reciprocal relationship between leaders and followers. This style becomes the means to produce and enhance this reciprocal relationship. The essence of leadership is to get something done. How those things get done can vary from person to person.

The Bible identifies many different leaders who accomplished great things in the Kingdom of God. A closer examination reveals that many of those biblical leaders reacted and responded in different ways. Some were relations or people-oriented and others were task-oriented. When mixed with active (outgoing) and reflective (passive/reserved) types, the DISC model is defined.

Another definition of leadership is "the art of creating a working climate that inspires others to achieve extraordinary goals and level of performances." The leader's main objective is to clearly communicate the vision to the team. An exceptional leader knows that sharing the mission will get everyone involved with the vision. Scripture reinforces this truth in Habakkuk 2:2, "Write the vision and make it plain on tablets, that he may run who reads it."

Effective leaders discover that mentoring and discipling are essential for developing the success of the entire team. By letting group members outline the mission statement for tasks, the leader motivates the group to build a diverse team of dedicated followers. *Followership* may be defined as the ability to effectively follow the directives and support the efforts of a leader to maximize a structured organization.

Nevertheless, the world system views followership as being feeble. The solution to inspiring followers is explaining the value of the group's vision. Leaders and followers become powerful when they listen and value the opinions or concerns of others. Research supports the fact that followers and leaders enjoy working together when they are happy with the group's values and missions.

Trust becomes the key factor in working with the different personality styles on the team. Many times, enabling trust in a group is dependent upon the level of discipling and mentoring which a leader does. Knowing the difference between mentoring and discipling becomes a vital component of the overall team's success.

16

Mentoring & Discipling: Should I Make More Like Me?

"The pen is mightier than the sword."
—Edward Bulwer-Lytton

Words are powerful. In 1839, Edward Bulwer-Lytton coined the phrase for a play which says, "The pen is mightier than the sword." However, the thought was not unique to him. As early as 406 BC, the Greek poet Euripides said, "The tongue is mightier than the blade." Pre-dating all that is Genesis 1:3 when the Lord demonstrated the true power of words and SAID, "Let there be light," and there was light.

Two words that contain infinite power are **discipling** and **mentoring**. These are two words of action and change. Their reach is beyond time and space. These words have the power to last forever.

However, these words are not interchangeable and will produce different results. **Mentoring** focuses on helping others learn and is follower-centric. Mentoring is based upon relationship and focuses on leaders working with followers to be all they can be. The mentor's goal is to help followers accomplish their own plans. I attended a church where the Pastor's vision was, "Equipping Believers to Fulfill Their Destiny;" this is the essence of mentoring.

Discipling produces a different outcome. Discipling is leader-centric where a person is learning from the leader (or master) and wants to be like the leader. Therefore, followers give up their plans in order to take on the vision or purpose of the leader. This can be seen in Scripture where Jesus told His followers to go and make disciples:

> *Then the eleven disciples went away into Galilee, to the mountain which Jesus had appointed for them. When they saw Him, they worshiped Him; but some doubted. And Jesus came and spoke to them, saying, "All authority has been given to Me in heaven and on earth. Go therefore and make disciples of all the nations, baptizing them in the name of the Father and of the Son and of the Holy Spirit, teaching them to observe all things that I have commanded you; and lo, I am with you always, even to the end of the age." Amen* (Matthew 28:16-20).

The Greek word used here for "disciples" is *mathetes* which is used over 250 times in the New Testament. *Mathetes* is like an apprentice in modern times. These followers of Jesus served as His apprentices.

As Christian leaders, it takes wisdom to be able to determine which method to use in developing followers. Both roles are valuable, but produce different outcomes. Mentoring produces a diverse group of people each accomplishing the vision God gave them; discipling produces a group which looks, speaks, and acts the same as they pursue a common vision.

The Apostle Paul encouraged Christians in 1 Corinthians 11:1 to "imitate me just as I also imitate Christ." Even with a strong "D" personality, Paul understood the need for discipleship in the lives of his followers and wanted them to become like him. Dr. Cornelius Bekker from Regent University identified four important aspects of discipleship:

- Followers must desire to learn and be like the master or leader.
- Followers must say no to their own plans and die to self.
- They take up the vision of the leader.
- They take up the quest of the leader.

However, discipling does not need to be a face-to-face encounter. Discipling can be a self-study process. The Apostle Paul is still producing disciples today through his writings and teachings.

On the other hand, mentoring requires a face-to-face encounter. Since mentoring relies upon relationship, there is an implication of time being spent with the person being mentored. General Dwight Eisenhower was once asked by Edgar Puryear how a person can be developed as a decision maker. The General replied that the key was to be around people who made decisions and rely on them as mentors.

It is important to emphasize that mentoring requires that one-on-one time to be effective. However, discipling can be accomplished through the study of the documents left behind.

The Transformative Personality

The goal of this book is to understand your personality and to help you control it rather than your personality controlling you. A personality style or trait should never be used as an excuse for poor behavior. Our God is a transforming God and He wants to transform our personality as we grow from glory to glory.

Transformation is about change. To be a transformational leader is to motivate the members in the group to accomplish more than they originally intended or even thought possible. **The Oxford Dictionary** defines "transformation" as "a thorough or dramatic change in form or appearance." Romans 12:2 states that we, as Christians, are to be transformed by the renewing of our minds.

The Greek word for "transformed" is *metamorphoo*. The English word "metamorphosis" comes from this word, and it means to change-from within. A transformational leader must produce an internal change in their followers. This internal change is produced by renewing the mind.

The transformative process is dependent upon this renewing of the mind. Followers have to learn to think differently; in other words, controlling their personality rather than their personality controlling them. This transformative process is dependent upon the follower being where the real decisions get made in the group.

Within transformative leadership, it is vision, purpose, beliefs, and other aspects of the organizational culture that are of prime importance. Producing the right team from the right mix of personalities is vital to the success of the team and the accomplishment of the tasks. This principle is true whether it's in a corporate setting, on a church committee, or in a child's playgroup.

Mentoring and/or discipling come into play when dealing with the individual members of the team. The individual members each step up to produce their transformed personality by renewing the mind.

One of the primary keys to leadership is the ability to make decisions and to get things accomplished. Transformative leaders are decision makers, and their leadership is contingent upon the ability to make the right decision at the right time.

A popular phrase in the military says, "The only constant is change." Michael Dell, the founder of Dell Computers, states that the, "The only constant thing about our business is that everything is changing." If no change is needed, then very little leadership is required; that entity would just need a manager.

To maintain the status quo requires little effort or focus. According to the online **Merriam-Webster Dictionary**, "change" can be a verb or a noun and basically means to make something different. Simply stated, without change there would be little to zero innovation and everything would stay the same. Very few things would move forward since most things would be moving in a circle. The vast majority of modern day technological advances are the product of change.

The transformational leader should be a catalyst to produce change in an organization. The challenge is being able to catalyze or spark change for the good of the organization. That requires research, time, and proper planning for building the right team. Change may happen quickly. However, positive change requires research, time, wisdom, and knowledge. Without the required amount of time and research, change may not be for the good of the organization.

Building the proper team through using the DISC model of personality styles becomes a vital component to producing valuable and effective change for any group or organization—be it at home or at work.

18

SO WHY DO I DO THE THINGS I DO?

> *Therefore He says: "When He ascended on high, He led captivity captive, And gave gifts to men"* (Ephesians 4:8).

Like all good fathers, our Heavenly Father wants His children to succeed in life. No father wants their kids to be unhappy, unproductive, or unsuccessful. Failure is not an option in the minds of good fathers when it comes to their kids. How much more does our Heavenly Father want good things for us?

> *"Ask, and it will be given to you; seek, and you will find; knock, and it will be opened to you. For everyone who asks receives, and he who seeks finds, and to him who knocks it will be opened. Or what man is there among you who, if his son asks for bread, will give him a stone? Or if he asks for a fish, will he give him a serpent? If you then, being*

> *evil, know how to give good gifts to your children, how much more will your Father who is in heaven give good things to those who ask Him!* (Matthew 7:7-11).

Most gifts given by the Lord need to be developed and the personality gift is no exception. Our personalities start out much like a newborn infant: dependent and in need of development. However, the personality gift is also one of the first gifts to be given in order to prepare you for the plan and future that the Lord has for your life. Remember we said earlier that 85% of a child's personality is formed by the time they reach the age of five. We must learn to control our personalities rather than allowing them to control us, and we, as leaders, have a responsibility to teach others to do the same thing.

My goal in writing this book is to help you understand how your personality can govern your interactions, feelings, and decisions. The DISC model is a tool that can be used to help you determine the general category of your personality traits. With this information, you can learn more about yourself—why you do the things you do. In addition, you can also come to a better understanding of others—whether it's your spouse, children, or other family members or maybe it's your co-worker, someone you supervise, or even your boss. Life is made up of relationships and the more tools that you have to help navigate that often complex ground of human interactions, the better.

Once you determine your base personality with the DISC model, you can determine your secondary traits with a little observation. As I mentioned earlier, a "D" personality has certain traits of being dominant, demanding, and determined, but when mixed with the secondary traits of an "I" we see the "D" bent in a different direction. You might look at it as the secondary trait seasons your primary trait with grace and helps you be a better, more well-rounded person.

There are personality profiles which exist out in the marketplace which can ask you survey questions to help you determine your personality blend or you can just ask yourself: are you active towards tasks or people? Are you an introvert (passive/reflective) or an extrovert (active)? The answers to these questions will help you narrow down your own unique personality blend.

Through the Biblical persons we examined, we can see how the various personalities look in the life of a person. It's one thing to read a list of bulleted characteristics, but it's another thing to examine a life looking at how their personality affects their interactions, feelings, and decisions. You can probably look around your own life and start to identify personalities.

My "CS" daughter came home from school annoyed with a person in her class, but now that she's equipped with the DISC tool, she can use reason to understand. As an example, she wanted to continue working on a group project as a "C" would want because she's all about the task, but her classmate wanted to chit-chat. Realizing that her classmate is probably an "I" personality gives her understanding, and understanding decreases frustration and helps her function better in her team to get the job done.

Renown scientist, Dr. Albert Einstein said, "Peace cannot be kept by force; it can only be achieved by understanding." As Christians, we are instructed to pursue peace. The DISC personality model helps us pursue peace with the people in our lives. One of my favorite authors is Dr. Stephen Covey and one of his habits for highly effective people is to seek first to understand and then to be understood. Understanding personalities becomes a key piece to understanding people.

They say opposites attract so when I married my wife, my "DI" came together with her "CS" so that our union now benefits from all four of the personality traits. Was this a challenge before we understood about personalities? It could have been. However, with knowledge of DISC it has worked great in our marriage because where I am weak, she is strong; where she is weak, I am strong. I'm not trying to make my wife like me and she's not trying to make me like her; we can appreciate the unique giftings that each of us possesses, and we're both better for it. That's the same way it is with building a team! Utilizing all the benefits of each personality trait will help you to build a well-rounded team that can accomplish goals while each team member finds personal fulfillment. Research shows that there are fewer turnovers when people are personally fulfilled; it is a natural human pursuit, and understanding personalities will help achieve that fulfillment.

The understanding of personalities becomes the answer to why do I do the things that I do! It is my earnest prayer that you utilize this knowledge to be a productive team member, productive citizen, and to enjoy your life's journey!

SOURCES

Bass, B. M. (2008). *The Bass Handbook of Leadership*. New York: Free Press.

Winston, B. E., & Patterson, K. (2006). "An Integrative Definition of Leadership." International Journal of Leadership Studies, 1(2), 6-66.

Yukl, G. A. (2009). *Leadership in Organizations* (7th ed.). Englewood Cliffs, NJ: Prentice Hall.

DARRELL PARSONS

DARRELL PARSONS is a military officer, Bible teacher and businessman. He lives with his wife and daughter in Virginia. Darrell has been a Christian for almost forty years and continues to be involved in ministry as he has for the last twenty-five years.

Darrell has been involved in team building through understanding personalities in varied capacities. Throughout his career, he has worked in educational, military, church, and business environments.

The first book he authored is entitled, **Release Your Words—Impact Your World**. Currently, Darrell is a doctoral candidate at Regent University studying Strategic Leadership.

From his varied background and training, Darrell offers a unique insight into developing leaders and helping people reclaim their voices.

Parsons Publishing House
Your Voice Your World ™

SURVIVING THE CHALLENGES OF TRANSITION
by Dr. Gerald Doggett

Dr. Doggett exhorts the reader to not let their past dictate their future. He provides exciting nuggets which include: It's OK to Remain A Chair!, Your Dream Will Attract Favor & Warfare, God Restores Everything That Has Been Lost!, Sometimes You Need to Have A Party! $12.95.

PORTRAIT OF A PASTOR'S HEART
A Manual on Caring for the Sheep
by Bishop Gerald Doggett

This book is a must for pastors, elders, students & laymen who want to learn how to care for the flock of God. Bishop Gerald Doggett paints a rare and intimate portrait covering TOPICS such as: Spirit of a Finisher, The Necessity of the Divine Call and A Beautiful Portrait of Preparation. $12.95.

WHY DO I DO THE THINGS I DO?
Understanding Personalities
by Darrell Parsons

In this insightful book, Darrell Parsons identifies the four primary types of personalities and how they interact together. As you grow in understanding, you will gain the tools you need for developing successful relationships in all areas of your life. $10.95.

SILENCING THE ENEMY WITH PRAISE
by Pastor Robert Gay

In this book, you will learn what God's Word says about the power of praise to: destroy the strongholds of Satan; bring healing, deliverance, and restoration; release the prophetic word; win the victory in spiritual warfare; and drive out demonic principalities. $11.95.

70 REASONS FOR SPEAKING IN TONGUES
by Bishop Bill Hamon

Over 600 million Christians have received the Holy Spirit gift of tongues, and 95% of Spirit-baptized Christians only utilize 10% of the benefits of speaking in tongues. Learn how to use your spirit language to activate more faith and increase God's love and power within your life and ministry (216 pages). $14.95.

30 DAYS TO A BETTER PRAYER LIFE
by Pastor Nora King

Nora King offers fresh revelation and practical teaching to help you experience the release of God's power. You will learn daily how to improve your prayer life and enter God's presence through these simple principles. You don't have to struggle in prayer any longer! $11.95.

RELEASE YOUR WORDS—IMPACT YOUR WORLD
by Darrell Parsons

Your words can make a difference! God has placed treasures inside you; learn to release them to influence your world. In this book, Darrell Parsons challenges you to use your voice to impact the world around you today. $9.95.

THE EFFECTIVE PRAISE & WORSHIP LEADER
by Dr. Ron Kenoly

What is a good worship leader? What does a pastor want in a worship leader? Use this book as a measuring stick for the anointed person you want to become. From his vast experience, Ron Kenoly shares insight into the office of the worship leader. $10.95.

The PRIORITY OF PRAISE & WORSHIP
by Dr. Ron Kenoly

Through this book, you will receive proven answers to common and uncommon issues from one of the nation's leading worship authorities. Each chapter is designed to take you to a higher level of excellence in your worship experience. $12.95.

LIFTING HIM UP
by Ron Kenoly & Pastor Dick Bernal

Worship leader Ron Kenoly teams up with pastor, Dick Bernal, in this practical guide to praise and worship. You'll learn Bible how to enter into the Lord's presence, plus gain insight into the scriptural role of praise and worship in your life and church. $12.95.

REVELATION: BEHIND THE VEIL
by Rev. Laurin E. Young

The book of Revelation has intrigued people through the years. Rev. Laurin Young shares his years of study in this chapter by chapter commentary on the Apocalypse. The rich spiritual truths serve as a "layman's commentary" and a good reference tool for teachers. $14.95.

CAPTURING THE HEART OF GOD
Pleasing the Father in Everyday Life
by Diane Parsons

God created man for His good pleasure. Make it your goal today to do those things which please God. This book contains practical tips on how capturing the heart of God and becoming His delight every day. $10.95.

WITH EVERY BEAT OF MY HEART - A Weekly Devotional
by Jeff North

Every Beat of My Heart takes the reader to a place where inspirational stories and poems stay upon their hearts and lips throughout the day. This book offers a practical message with a godly foundation to encourage, motivate and bring comfort (224 pages). $14.95.

MEMOIR TO MY BOSOM BUDDY
Journal of My Walk With Breast Cancer
by Janet Bergdoll

Like thousands of other women, Janet was diagnosed with breast cancer. As a registered nurse, she underwent treatment by the book, and she journalled through her diagnosis, treatment, and recovery. The result is an inspirational book about her walk with breast cancer. $12.95.

MOUNTAIN VIEW - A Photo Collection
by Doris Beets

Contained in these pages is a pictorial discovery of a community where splendor is exemplified. Doris Beets attempts to give you a glimpse of the world that captured her heart over 75 years ago. $29.95.